Horror Haiku
And Other Poems

A. F. Stewart

Horror Haiku and Other Poems

A. F. Stewart

Copyright © 2016 A. F. Stewart

All rights reserved.

ISBN: 978-1-365-42077-1

No part of this book may be reproduced or distributed in any printed or electronic form without permission of the author.
This is a work of fiction. All characters and events portrayed in this book are a product of the author's imagination. Any resemblance to persons living or dead is purely coincidental.

Cover design by A. F. Stewart
Original artwork courtesy of Pixabay

Photos courtesy of Pixabay

DEDICATION

This book was inspired by the dark and deadly hashtag event #HorrorHaikuesday on Twitter. So a great thank you to its creator @horror_made and all my horror peeps on Twitter.

CONTENTS

1 Haiku of Horror   1
2 Poetry in Red and Black   79
3 About the Author   113

Velvet petals, frail

against the storm –

they decay

fall like rain, like death

Haiku of Horror

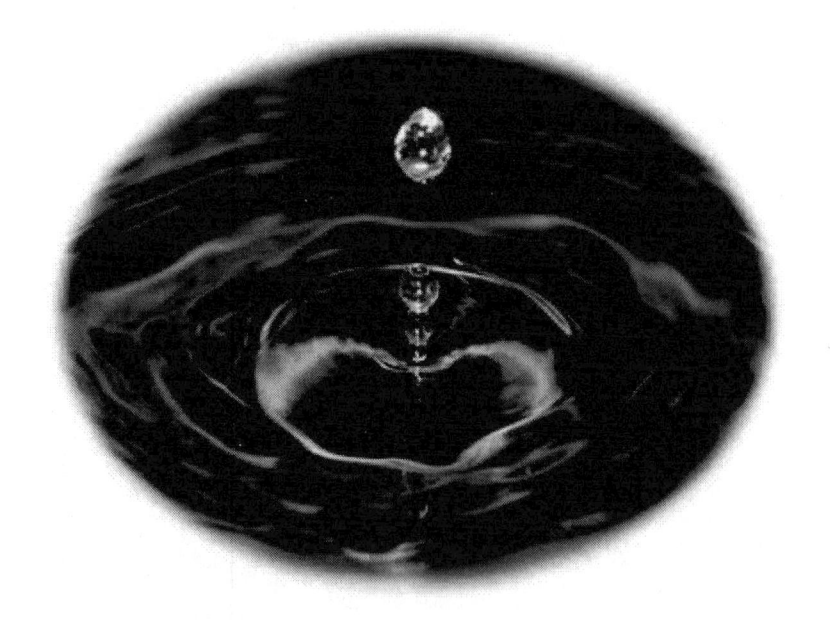

A. F. STEWART

HORROR HAIKU

In stillness, a sound

catch the cacophony vein—

drip, drip, dripping blood

A. F. STEWART

HORROR HAIKU

Creep insanity

along the cobblestones dark

Sharp blade, carve a smile

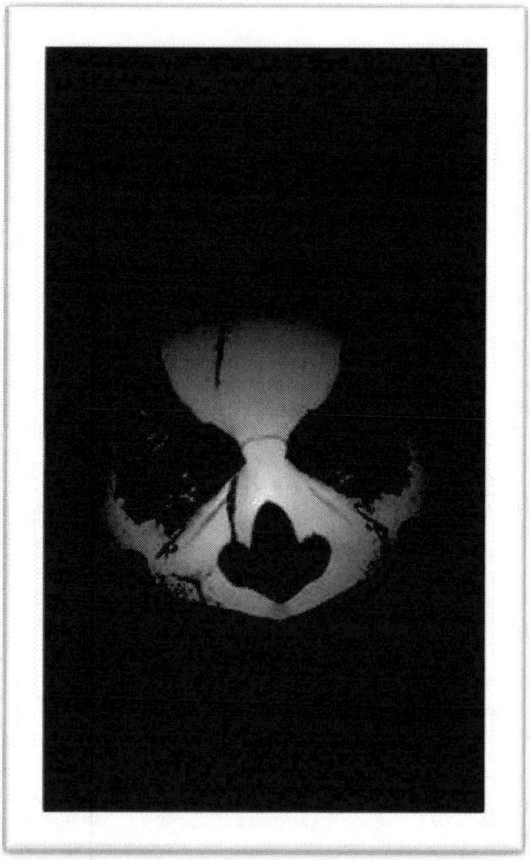

HORROR HAIKU

Darkened carnival

Quiet time—don't slip in blood

The red-nosed clown smiles

A. F. STEWART

HORROR HAIKU

Oh, accursed fate

of fang and claw—beast unleashed

on the moonlit night

HORROR HAIKU

Faint breath past silence

abandoned in the darkness

Nowhere left to run

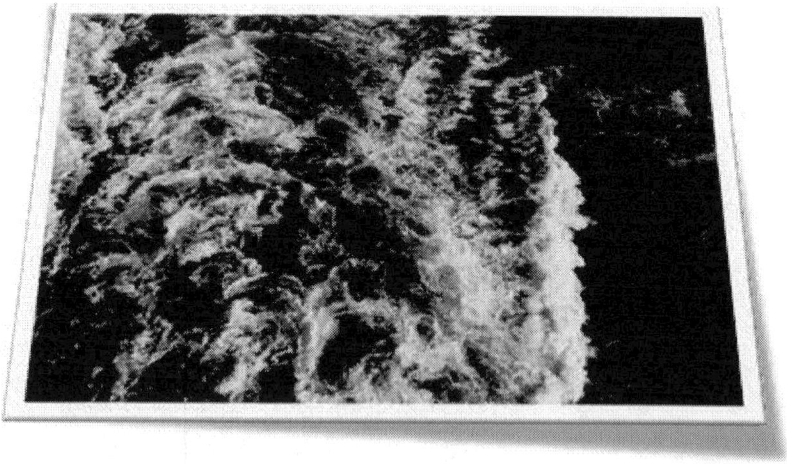

HORROR HAIKU

Dark waters—falling

down, down swallowed by cold depths

tentacles reaching

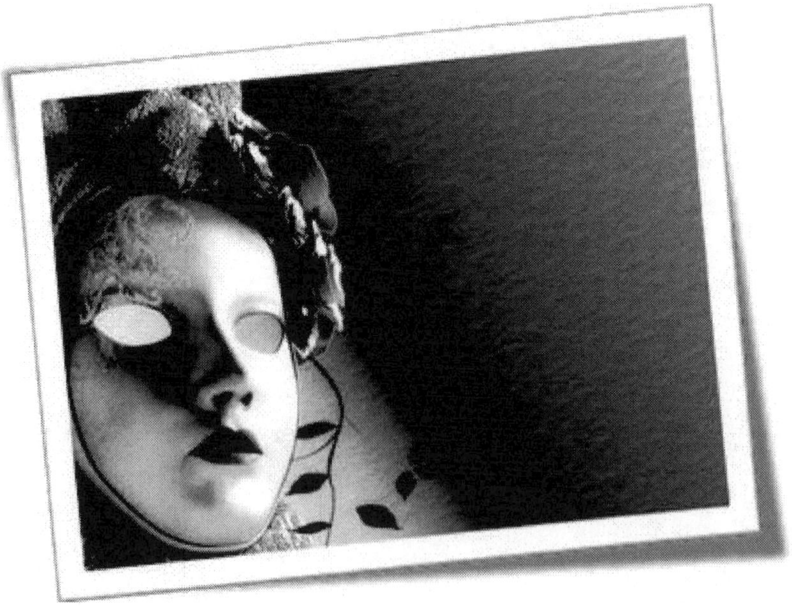

HORROR HAIKU

Red masks and music

dance the dark streets, tempting smiles

blood—lost in shadows

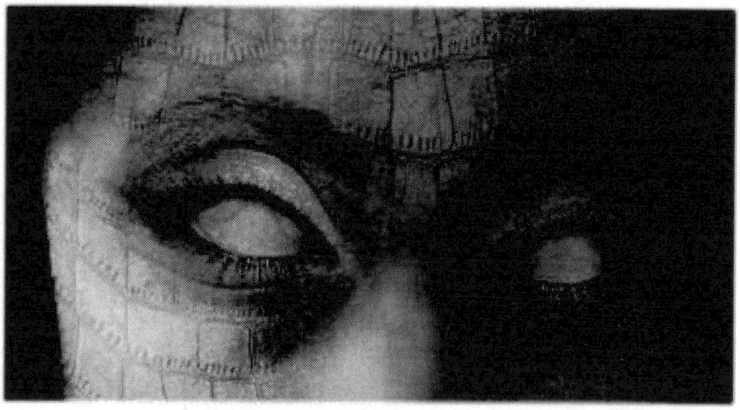

HORROR HAIKU

She waits for her love,

pale, trembling, silent. She walks—

among the undead

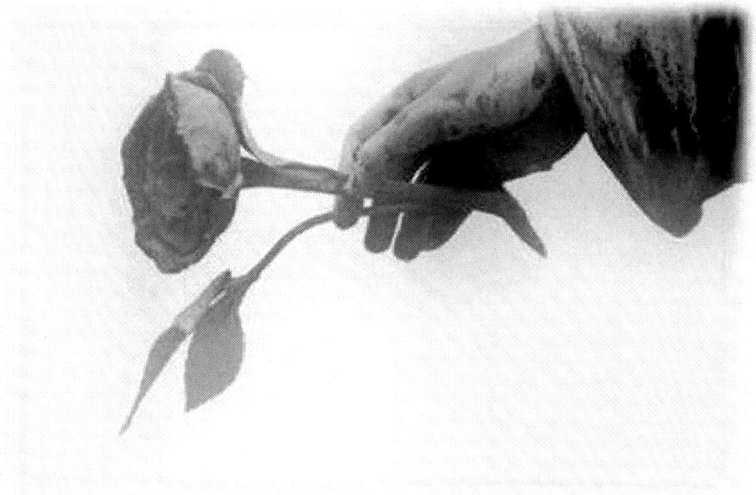

HORROR HAIKU

Grey, ghostly spectre

moonlight rising from the grave…

Revenge will be hers

A. F. STEWART

HORROR HAIKU

Waiting beneath—still

it listens, its hunger gnaws

Soon it will dig up

A. F. STEWART

HORROR HAIKU

Tick, tock. Time flows, slows.

Close your eyes. Nowhere to... hide.

Door opens. He's coming.

A. F. STEWART

HORROR HAIKU

Hark the Ides Of March

discontent sharpens the blade

blood spills on marble

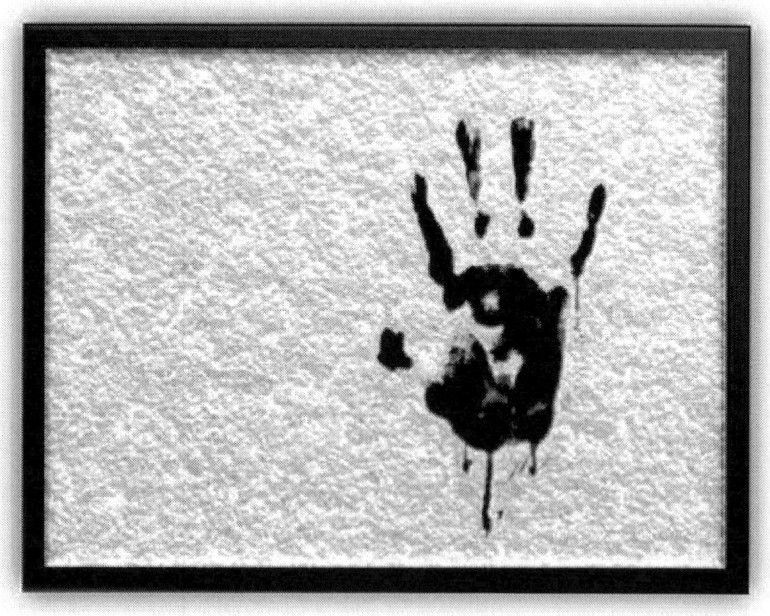

HORROR HAIKU

Darkest deep, unvoiced

beneath cracked civility

until the blood spills

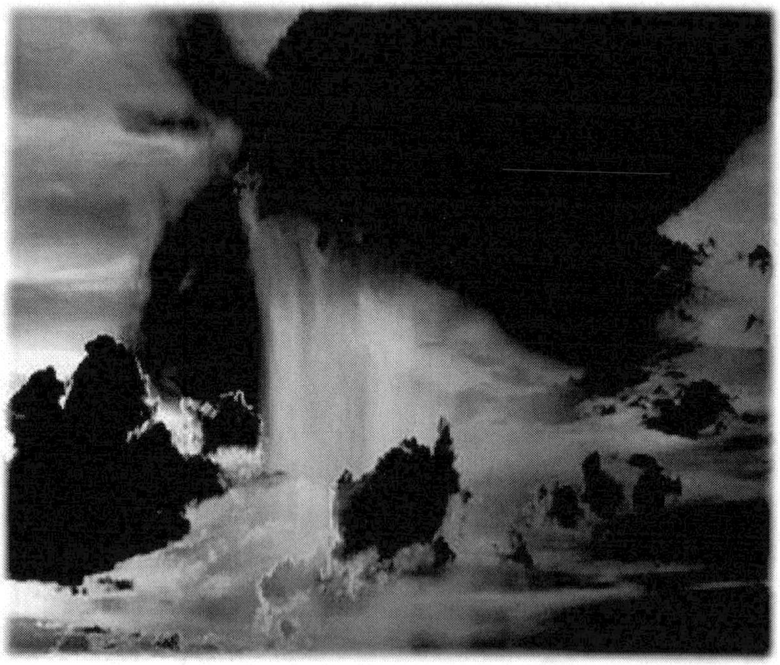

HORROR HAIKU

Sable sky caress

ardent touch of death tears

the glory world burns

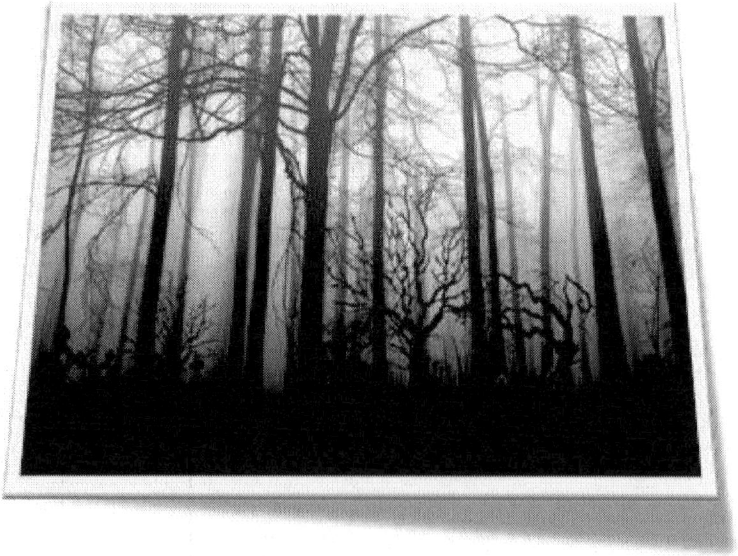

HORROR HAIKU

Dark, an icy chill

Where am I? It can't be—

I'm buried alive

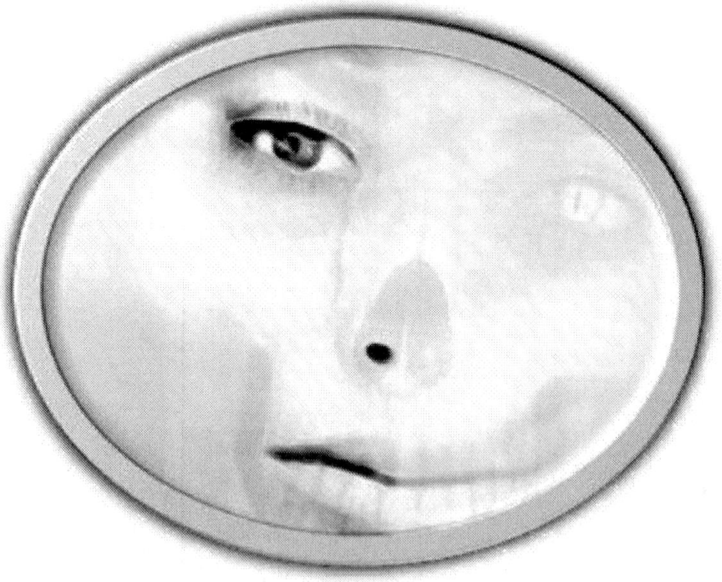

HORROR HAIKU

That old devil's smile

reflection in your mirror

blood drops on the glass

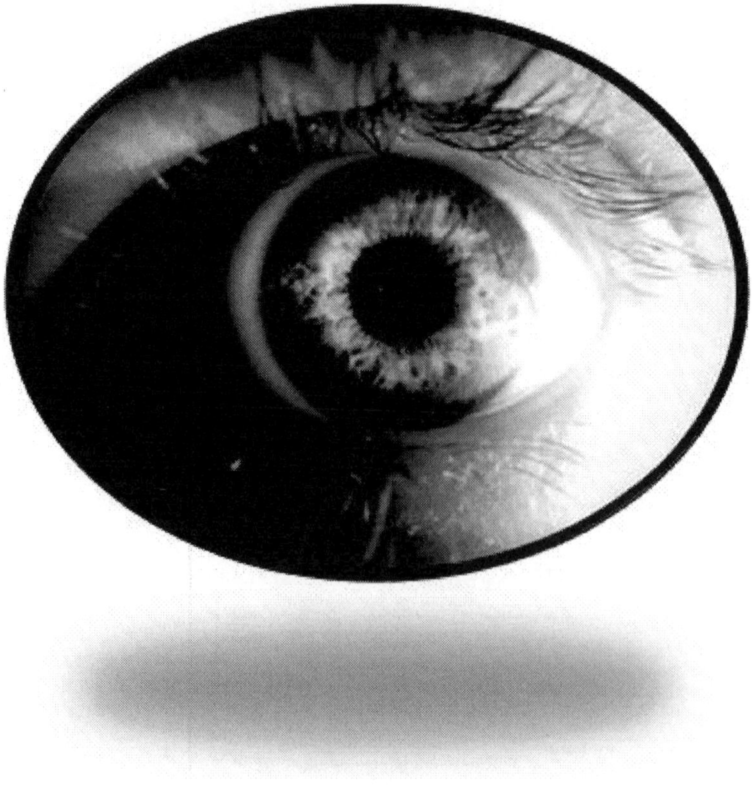

HORROR HAIKU

Monsters in the dark

Hide your eyes, shiver darling

I am the nightmare

A. F. STEWART

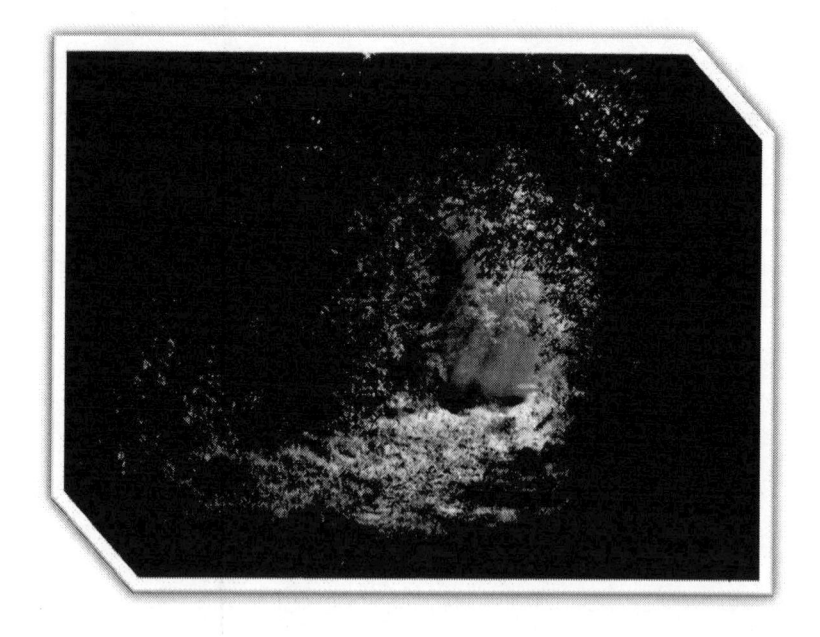

HORROR HAIKU

Black, the woodland night

where the faeries linger

with their knives so sharp

A. F. STEWART

HORROR HAIKU

London gaslight hiss

cobblestone shadows shiver

and the undead walk

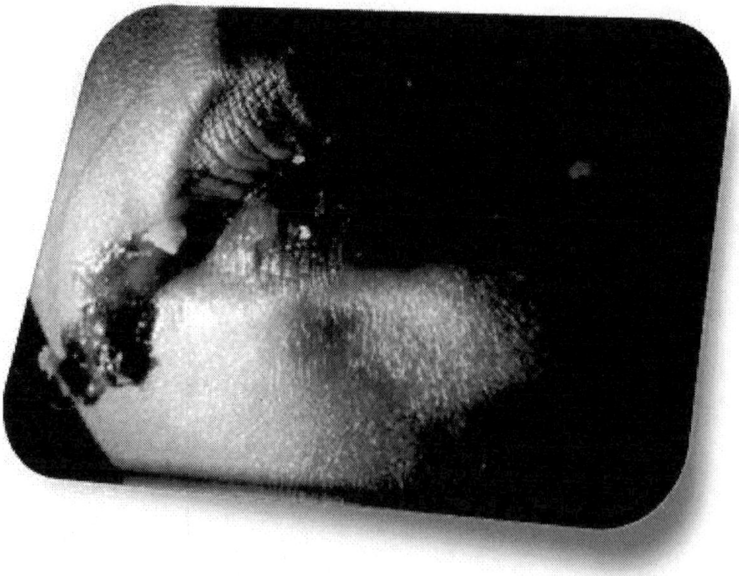

HORROR HAIKU

Crunching teeth—feasting

grinding bone, tearing the flesh

while their meals yet scream

A. F. STEWART

HORROR HAIKU

Black, are the still depths

of stars, the fathomless sea

In R'lyeh he waits

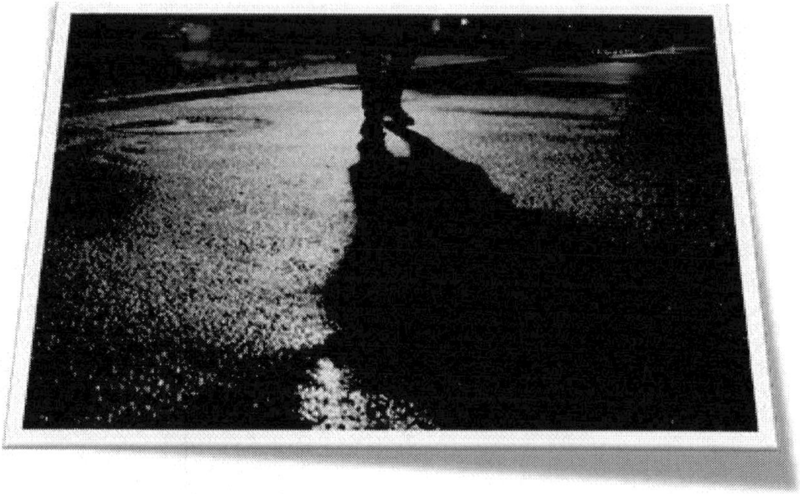

HORROR HAIKU

Heavy lies the night

It swallows me—I am lost

one more scream echoes

A. F. STEWART

HORROR HAIKU

Entwined in the bark

silent scream, petrified flesh

petals smell of blood

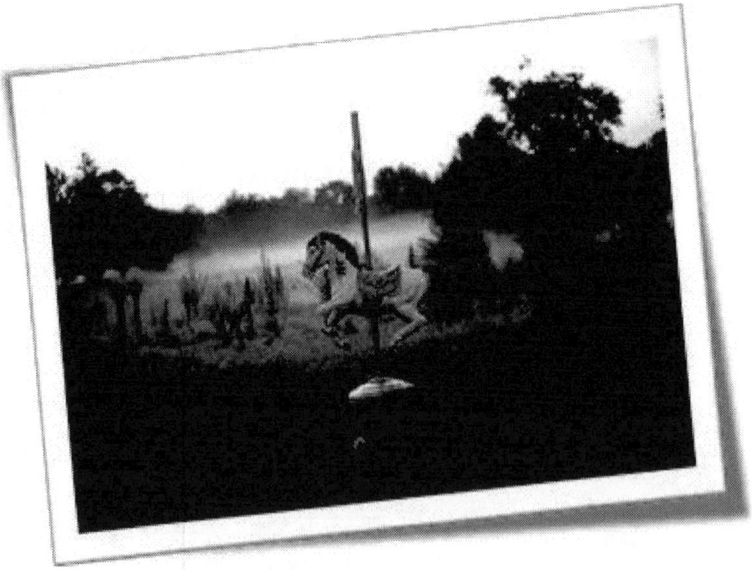

HORROR HAIKU

Shadows over rust

Forsaken carnival fun

mask the gate to Hell

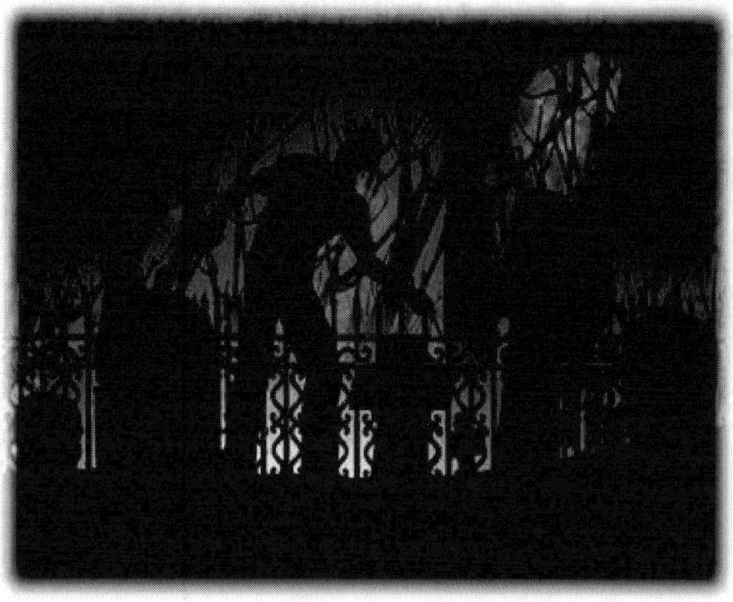

HORROR HAIKU

Mist in the graveyard

following footsteps beyond

shadows—not human

A. F. STEWART

HORROR HAIKU

Her pretty face smiles

until the front door closes

blood stains need cleaning

A. F. STEWART

HORROR HAIKU

Deja vu darkness

stalked down a bleak lonely street

Time resets for death

A. F. STEWART

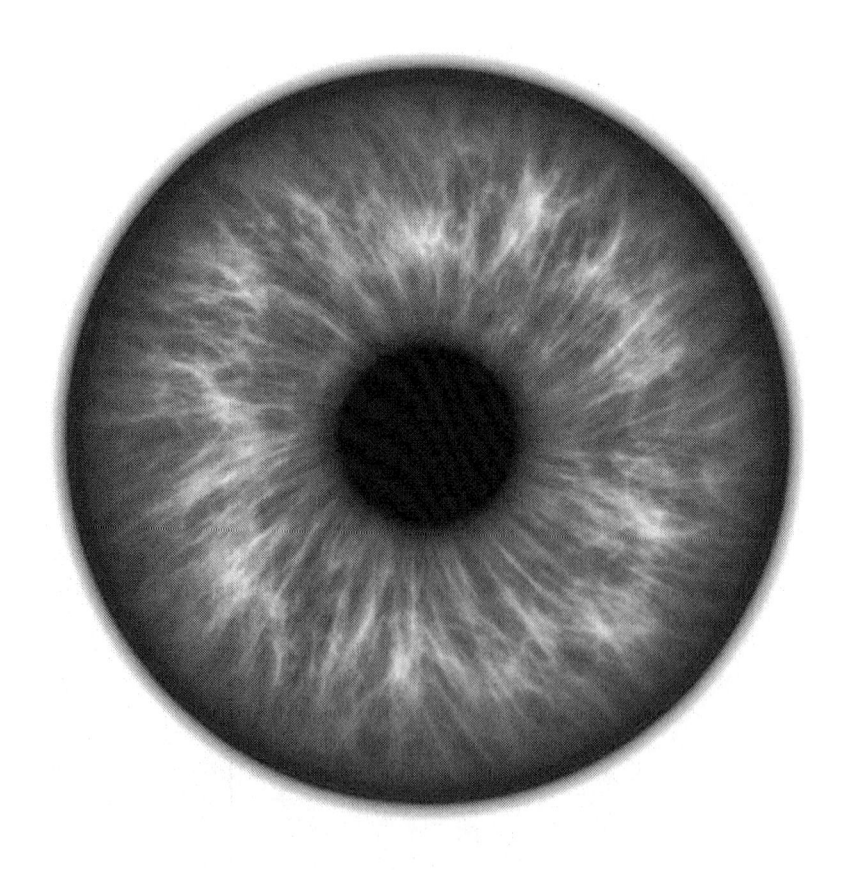

HORROR HAIKU

I can't see well. Pain.

My wife is holding something.

My eyeball. I scream.

HORROR HAIKU

Watch them standing guard

along the northern most wall

the dead hold the line

A. F. STEWART

HORROR HAIKU

Hush, little baby

now so still—you'll cry no more

Your Daddy came home

A. F. STEWART

HORROR HAIKU

See the pretty homes

Along came plague—empty rows

Everyone is dead

A. F. STEWART

HORROR HAIKU

Little flower, pale

the petals crushed, lightly brushed

in the poison pie

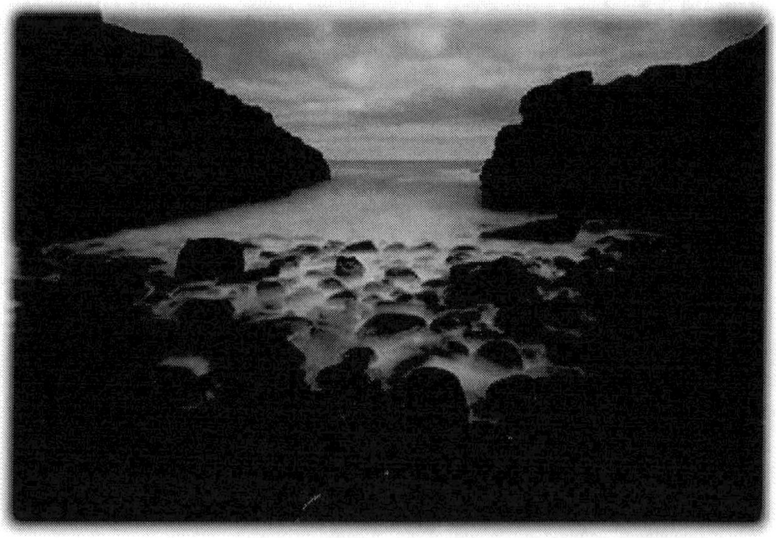

HORROR HAIKU

Wandering sailor,

Can you hear their charming song?

Too close—mermaids feast

A. F. STEWART

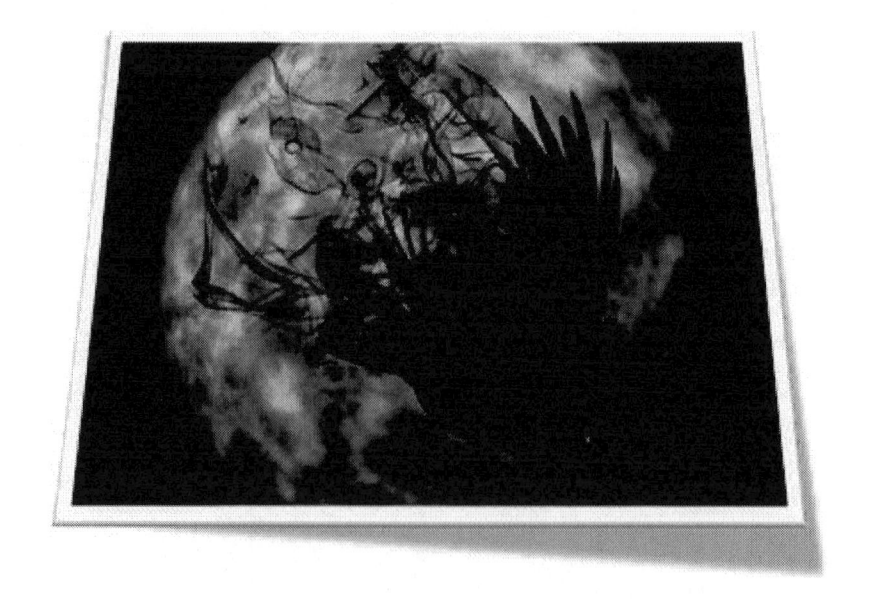

HORROR HAIKU

The night lies quiet

Still, under the heavens bright

Death comes on moonlight

A. F. STEWART

HORROR HAIKU

Alone, surrounded

by the dead. You are waiting...

Come, apocalypse

A. F. STEWART

HORROR HAIKU

Secluded, it waits

cold, damp pulsing growth, it creeps

Into light—it feeds.

A. F. STEWART

HORROR HAIKU

An empty midnight

darkness—no one left alive

Why are there voices?

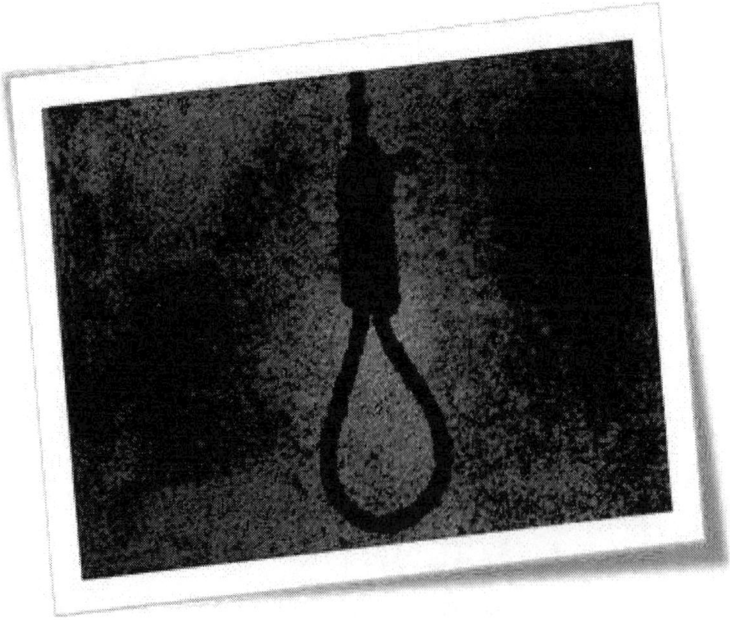

HORROR HAIKU

Hanging man will swing

as gallows creak and wind howls

Hanging man won't die

Poetry in Black and Red

A. F. STEWART

Artful Circumstance

visionary reflection

conduit of imagined sighs

sweet finite whisper

of a Botticelli brushstroke

in impasto crimson

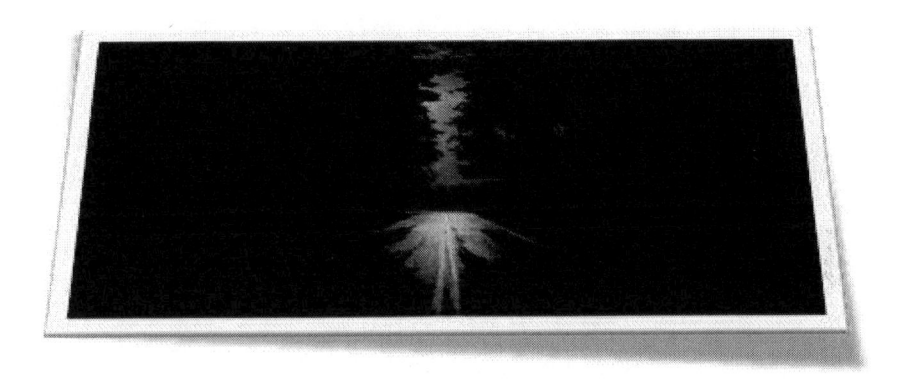

Beneath the Surface

The shadows quiver,

after sunrise

as the day prepares

to banish the night

But an ache lingers,

a ranting echo

with a purpose

The town sign still stands

A faded yellow,

from happier times

When it used to be

a place to laugh,

a place to learn

a place to live

Now, those days

only memories can recall

The town stands empty,

barricaded in isolation

a memorial cross

to tell its tragedy

Beware

Beware the whispers, on the darkest night

that creep amongst those shadows cast

their secrets told to the moon so bright

Words arcane, raised to winged flight

secrets shrieked, from unhallows past

Beware the whispers, on the darkest night

Spectral chattel, nattering twisted spite
venom spewed, malevolence asked,
their secrets told to the moon so bright

Skin to prickle, the air twisted blight
intentions, misgivings, nothing outlasts
their secrets told to the moon so bright

Shut your ears, and cower in fright
your eyes averted, your soul aghast
Beware the whispers, on the darkest night

Run, run, lest you conjoin their plight,
run poor wretch, every step your last
Beware the whispers, on the darkest night
their secrets told to the moon so bright

Black Tears

Salted drops fall

amidst the garden

stains on the narcissus

petals wilted damp

They fall like shadows

silhouettes of inky grief

chasing warm ashes

satiating a funeral urn

In the far distance

the ringing church bell

a clang for every tear

for emotions mired in tar

The hopeless tears fall

for morning memories,

smiles over warm cookies

and the life now empty

Brave New World

Steel and sinew

meshed under gears

Ironclad armour

dented and dinged

Guardian

Sentinel

Warden

A. F. STEWART

Watcher

It is the Vanguard

It is the Judge

Waiting…

Carnival of the Insane

I stare past the coloured lights, the façade,

to the laughing crowds, so amazed and awed.

Doesn't this carnival seem a tiny bit odd?

Yet, when the acts parade, I still applaud.

The barker bows, his grace ample and broad.

Then I notice his teeth; they appear sawed.

My first thought: I don't wish to be gnawed.

So I smile and nod, just smile and nod.

Wait, what? Oh my, is that clown clawed?

Oh dear, oh dear, I hope they don't maraud.

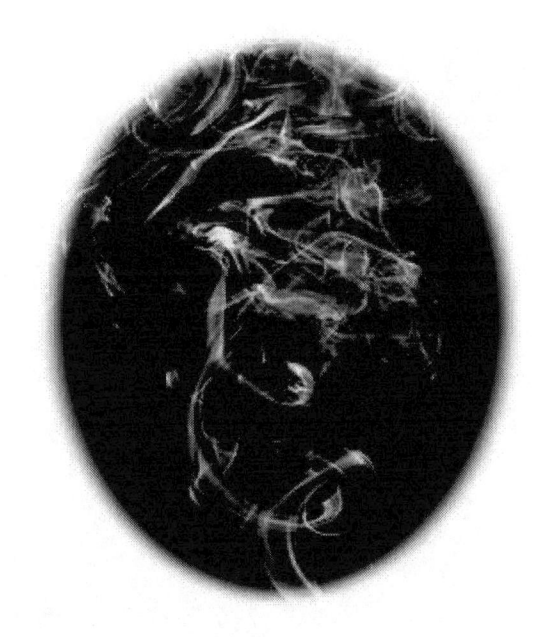

Dark Thread

Breathe

Whisper

one soft word

into the night

Death

A. F. STEWART

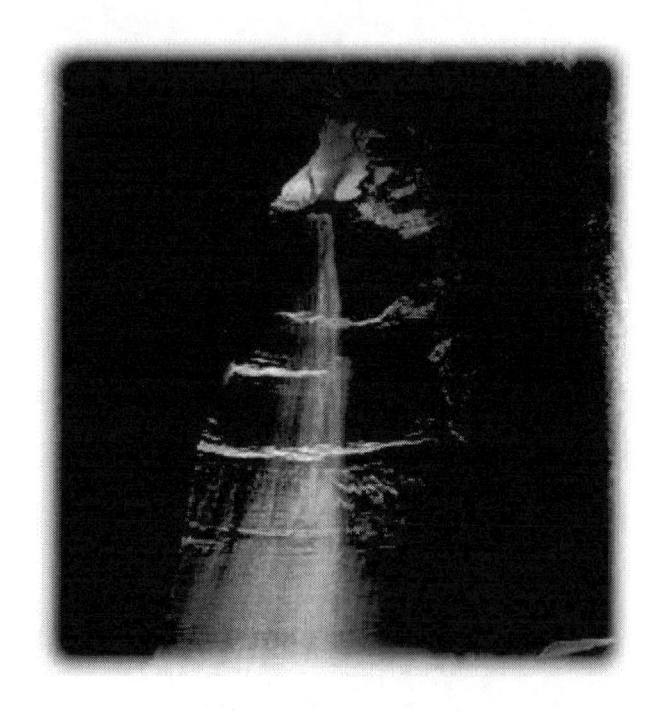

Do Not Disturb

Shift

Below

The Dark Earth

Hungry Old Gods

Wake

Fury Road

On the edge of the precipice

and stared into the desert

Shall all the eyes turn

or watch the world burn?

Inhaled the diesel fuel, the oil;

fire smoked beyond the sands

A. F. STEWART

Shall all the eyes turn

to watch the world burn?

Primal scream shook the land,

madness snaked into the brain

Shall all the eyes turn

and watch the world burn?

HORROR HAIKU

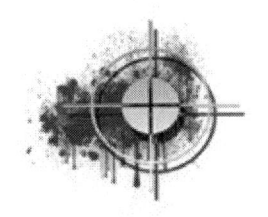

In the Cross Hairs

Don't breathe

on the dewdrop

of autonomy's illusion

They'll find you. They like fresh meat

Don't speak

an opinion voiced

calls down paroxysm

And leaves you bleeding on the street

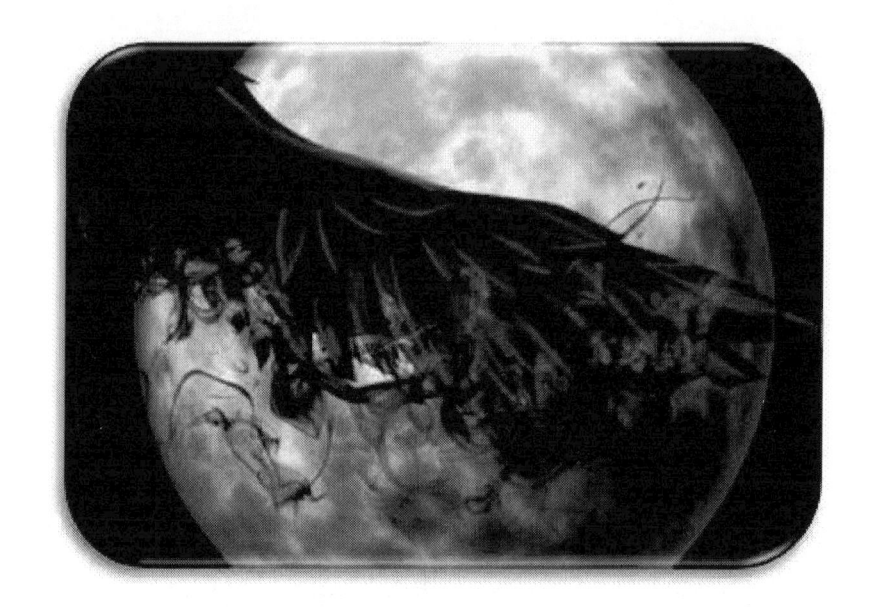

Midnight

Underneath the nocturnal moon

stir ghosts of sanguinary secrets

amidst the edges of sober reality

while an onyx raven takes wing

Voices sing a shadow's knell,

that melody of blood and grave,

HORROR HAIKU

to hail the stygian souls, *ascend*

while an onyx raven takes wing

Spinning the dusty devil's dance

above hoary and martyred bones

Rise, *oh*, rise, you hellion spawn

while an onyx raven takes wing

Come the thunder, crack the earth

in cackles of breath born laughter,

dredge forth those deathless screams

while an onyx raven takes wing

A. F. STEWART

Salutations to the End of the World

Descend the spiny umber rain

and rise the dust from fallow earth

Hollow shells will walk in the wake

Moon to sun and back again,

no matter the anguished cry, it comes—

Descend the spiny umber rain

HORROR HAIKU

Tarnished trinkets rust to nothing

while a thousand mouths, they hunger

and rise the dust from fallow earth

Red rivers run, the sad discarded

whispers silenced, no village left to raze

Hollow shells will walk in the wake

A. F. STEWART

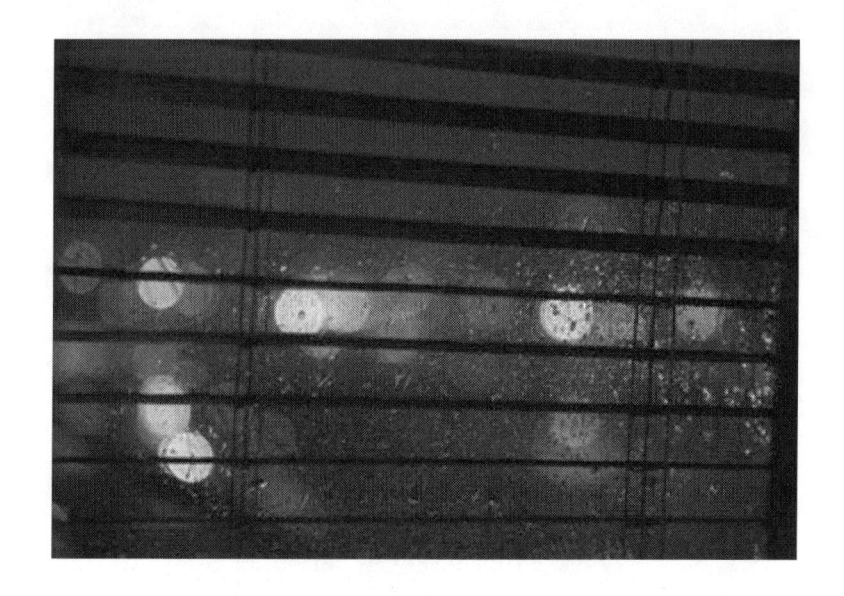

Step Into The Darkness

Are you broken?

Are you battered?

Are you shaking?

Are you shattered?

Do you hear the night-time screaming?

Out your name

In the hours when you're dreaming?

HORROR HAIKU

A waiting game

It's coming

Shriek

It's coming

Cower

It's coming

Flee

It's here

Hide

The Black Rose

She grips a black rose

a little too tight

the thorns bite

piercing skin

She welcomes the pain

HORROR HAIKU

and her blood flows

a scarlet river

down the stem

Through the Shutters

A meager, fading flicker of sunlight mingles

among the lengthening shadows on the floor.

The shutters pretend to bar the outside world;

these wooden slats only a façade of sanctuary

Among the lengthening shadows on the floor

rests the mark of a screaming, stolen mortality

snatched by circumstance and a world gone mad.

HORROR HAIKU

The shutters pretend to bar the outside world,

but it still seeps in, with all its dread and death.

It is simply a matter of time, before they come.

These wooden slats only a façade of sanctuary,

an ineffectual measure of delusional camouflage.

To ease the troubled mind, in advance of the end.

A. F. STEWART

Unhallowed Darkness

Sing the shadows

softly sleep

While the daughters

gently weep

Beyond the dark...

Beyond the night...

Stir the murky

mutely creep

HORROR HAIKU

With lost promises

calmly keep

Beyond the dark...

Beyond the night...

The wind, it whispers

wide and deep

The breath shall still

death will reap

Beyond the dark...

Beyond the night...

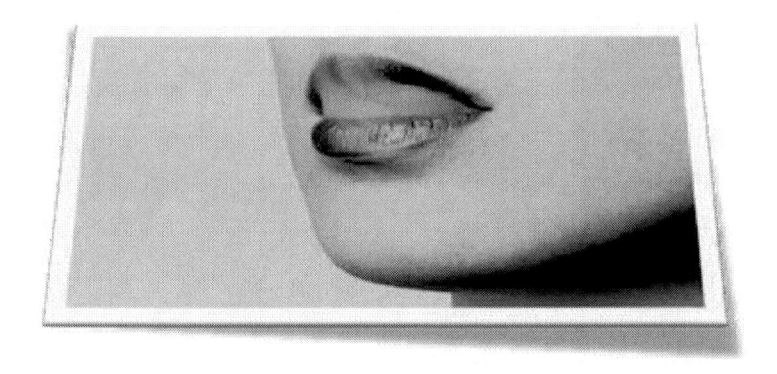

The Sound of Their Breathing

I watch the world inhale, exhale

each fragile breath so slight;

simple to asphyxiate, faces turning pale

I watch the world inhale, exhale

dreaming how to make them quail,

to quiver in fear, to scurry in flight

I watch the world inhale, exhale

each fragile breath so slight

HORROR HAIKU

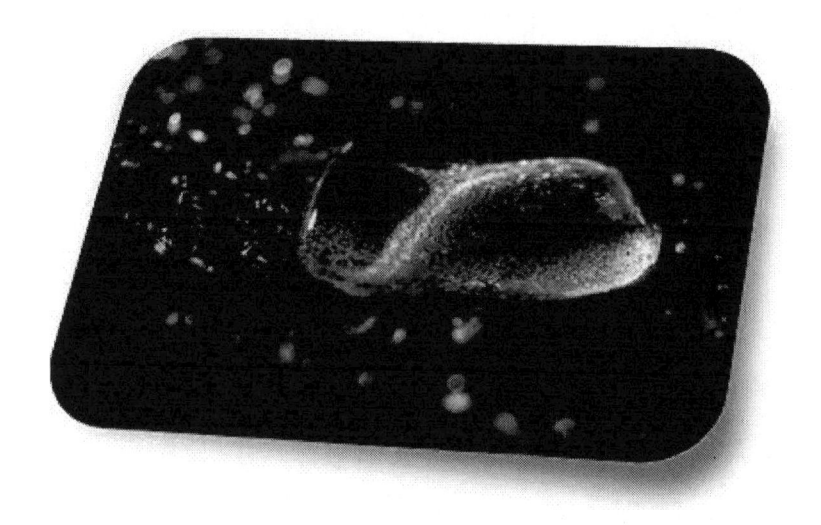

Dreaming Crimson

Inconsequential thoughts unravel,

stabbed by unbroken silence softly

bouncing off the velvet whisper

of the creeping obsidian shadow

And the rose red petals spill...

Shiver, shiver, the gold cup is empty

the raucous thunder shakes the rafters

The delicate sky shatters, shatters

with the sound of the rattling bones

The rose red flows against the night...

More Books by A. F. Stewart

Poetry:
Colours of Poetry
Reflections of Poetry
Shadows of Poetry
Tears of Poetry

Fiction:
Killers and Demons II: They Return
Fairy Tale Fusion
Gothic Cavalcade
Ruined City
Killers and Demons
Once Upon a Dark and Eerie...
Passing Fancies
Chronicles of the Undead
Inside Realms

Non-Fiction:
The Incomplete Guide to Action Movies

Multi-Author Anthologies:
Christmas Lites V
Christmas Lites IV
Christmas Lites III
Coffin Hop: Death by Drive-In
Mechanized Masterpieces
Legends and Lore
Beyond the Wail

ABOUT THE AUTHOR

A steadfast and proud sci-fi and fantasy geek, A. F. Stewart was born and raised in Nova Scotia, Canada and still calls it home. The youngest in a family of seven children, she always had an overly creative mind and an active imagination. She favours the dark and deadly when writing—her genres of choice being dark fantasy and horror—but she has been known to venture into the light on occasion. As an indie author she's published novellas and story collections, with a few side trips into poetry and non-fiction.
She is fond of good books, action movies, sword collecting, geeky things, comic books, and oil painting as a hobby. She has a great interest in history and mythology, often working those themes into her books and stories.

If you like to see more Haiku of Horror, please check out the #HorrorHaikuesday hashtag every Tuesday on Twitter. You can also check out the Horror Made blog each Tuesday to see the dark and lovely artwork by the talented Jeanette Andromeda.

Horror Made: https://horrormade.com/

Horror Made Artwork: https://society6.com/horrormade

Made in the USA
Columbia, SC
04 February 2024